IMAGES
of America

CASTLE GARDEN
AND BATTERY PARK

IMAGES
of America

CASTLE GARDEN
AND BATTERY PARK

Barry Moreno

ARCADIA
PUBLISHING

Published by Arcadia Publishing
Charleston, South Carolina

Printed in the United States of America

Library of Congress Catalog Card Number: 2006935748

For all general information contact Arcadia Publishing at:
Telephone 843-853-2070
Fax 843-853-0044
E-mail sales@arcadiapublishing.com
For customer service and orders:
Toll-Free 1-888-313-2665

Visit us on the Internet at www.arcadiapublishing.com

*This book is dedicated to Eric Byron, who drew my attention
to the archaeological treasures of Battery Park.*

CONTENTS

ACKNOWLEDGMENTS

I am very grateful to a number of people who very kindly provided some measure of assistance in the preparation of this book. First I should like to thank Erin Vosgien, my editor at Arcadia Publishing who saw the merit in this topic. At Castle Clinton National Monument, I am grateful for the encouragement of friends rangers Jim Cleckley, Daniel Prebutt, Peter Hom, Chris Kounkel, Laura Brennan, and chief of interpretation Steve Laise. At Ellis Island, I must thank my colleagues, Diana R. Pardue, Jeffrey S. Dosik, Eric Byron, Richard Holmes, and Kevin Daley. I am particularly grateful to ranger Dave McCutcheon, a splendid artist. Four of his paintings are showcased in this volume. I would also like to thank Rev. Fr. Peter Meehan, pastor of Our Lady of the Rosary Church; James Puppe of Fargo, North Dakota; Dr. Verlyn D. Anderson of Moorhead, Minnesota, who provided the Lutheran missionary's postcard reproduced on page 63—he also translated its mixed Swedish-Norwegian text into English; Dr. Blair O. Wolf of Arizona State University, for permission to use material on Charles H. Townsend from the *Condor*; rangers George Tonkin and Michael Amato; and former ranger George Hennessey.

INTRODUCTION

Castle Garden, one of New York's historic gems, lies in historic Battery Park and is one of the city's oldest structures. Yet its significance is now almost forgotten, for it has been wrapped in obscurity since 1950. Of course, one reason for its present obscurity is that it lost the name that made it famous—Castle Garden. Without it, most visitors—who almost exclusively come to purchase excursion tickets Liberty and Ellis Islands—would not connect it with the Castle Garden of legend. Today its current name of Castle Clinton hearkens back to its original but quite brief use as a fortress. This military phase was short and exceedingly quiet. When the structure ceased to be a fort and passed into civilian hands as Castle Garden, however, great things began to happen, and they continued for more than a century. These great moments in Castle Garden's history can be divided into three separate historic periods. The first lasted 30 years when Castle Garden dazzled New Yorkers and visitors alike as Manhattan's principal waterside gathering place for public celebrations, receptions, and concerts. The second phase was when it was transformed into the nation's very first immigrant landing station. During that period, eight million newcomers were registered there before being allowed to enter the United States. The third and last great moment came when Castle Garden served as the first and foremost municipal aquarium in America. Its specimens of sea life charmed millions of visitors for the next 45 years. Thus from 1824 to 1941, Castle Garden was a major institution in the cultural life of the city and even impacted the life of the United States as a whole.

Most people would agree that Castle Garden's use as an immigrant processing station was by far its greatest and most significant role in American history. After all, millions of Americans are descended from an ancestor who once passed through Castle Garden. New York State officials set up the facility with the intention of giving help and protection to foreigners and to see to it that they could easily continue their journey to destinations throughout the country. Of course, New Yorkers had other motives as well, probably the most important being the urgent need to reduce the numbers of foreigners that wound up in the slums, almshouses, and city hospitals. For it was realized that by assisting immigrants just after they had disembarked from ships, far fewer of them were likely to become victims of crime or unbidden poverty. Thus New York was eagerly looking for a solution. The result was the opening of the immigrant landing station at Castle Garden. The safety provided by delivering newcomers to Castle Garden was not perfect, but it still provided a greater measure of safety than had been the case before. A bureaucracy was then set up at the station, and departments to serve immigrants in other ways were also made available. These included a money exchange, a labor bureau, a restaurant, the city baggage delivery, a railroad ticket office, telegraph services, boardinghouse keepers, and missionaries. This volume gives an overview of some of these operations, as well as Castle Garden's years as a fort, a concert hall, and an aquarium. And, finally, the story of Battery Park is a continual leitmotif in the text, inviting readers to become better acquainted with its colonial and military past, as well as its long use as a city park.

CHRONOLOGY

1683	The Battery gets its name when cannons are placed there during this period.
1785	The Battery is landscaped and becomes Battery Park.
1807	Col. Jonathan Williams begins plans for a fortification in Battery Park.
1808	Architect John McComb handles the construction and designs the gateway.
1811	November 25: West Battery is completed, armed, and garrisoned.
1815	The War of 1812 ends; West Battery is renamed Castle Clinton.
1816	Castle Clinton becomes the headquarters of the United States Third Military District.
1820	The United States Third Military District is moved to Governors Island.
1821	The War Department abandons and demilitarizes Castle Clinton.
1822	March: Congress cedes the former fort to New York City.
1824	New York City renames it Castle Garden and leases it out for public events.
1824	Gaslights are installed, and Castle Garden opens in time for the Fourth of July.
1824	August 16: The Marquis de Lafayette visits Castle Garden.
1833	Pres. Andrew Jackson visits Castle Garden.
1839	The Castle Garden Theatre is established.
1841	Pres. John Tyler visits Castle Garden.
1842	Inventor Samuel Morse demonstrates the telegraph at Castle Garden.
1844–1845	A domed rotunda is added.
1847	Pres. James K. Polk is received at Castle Garden; opera bookings begin.
1850	September 11: P. T. Barnum presents opera star Jenny Lind at Castle Garden.
1851	Pres. Millard Fillmore makes a visit; Lola Montez performs there.
1852	Louis Kossuth makes his impassioned plea for Hungarian independence.
1855	Castle Garden becomes New York State's immigrant landing station.
1860	The Prince of Wales lands at Castle Garden, beginning his visit to America.
1876	July 9: Fire destroys several buildings.
1876	November 27 : Castle Garden reopens.
1880s	Emma Lazarus visits Castle Garden and Ward's Island and writes "The New Colossus."
1886	The Statue of Liberty is dedicated.
1890	April: The Castle Garden immigrant station closes.
1896	The New York Aquarium opens in Castle Garden.
1941	The aquarium closes and, next year, is demolished.
1950	Castle Garden legally becomes Castle Clinton National Monument.

One

THE BATTERY

THE BATTERY WATERFRONT. Castle Garden, now known as Castle Clinton National Monument, stands on the left, while the trees and crowds occupy much of the remainder of Battery Park. This photograph dates from around 1970. (National Park Service.)

BATTERY PARK FROM THE AIR. This shot was taken around 1958. Opened in 1785, Battery Park is New York City's second-oldest public park, after Bowling Green, which dates from 1733. As can be seen here, Battery Park is principally bounded, from left to right, by Battery Place and State Street. (New York Times.)

BATTERY PARK FROM STATE STREET. This picture was taken from the upper floor of a neighboring building and dates from about the late 1960s. (National Park Service.)

CASTLE CLINTON FROM THE AIR. This picture, showing the castle and the Eisenhower Mall, which leads to the junction of State Street and Battery Place with Broadway, dates from the mid-1960s.

DUTCH NIEUW AMSTERDAM, 1660. This model of the old Dutch colony of New Amsterdam represents the physical conditions of the town as it was in 1660. The wide road going north from Fort Amsterdam is the Heerewegh, called Broad Way in English. At the southern tip on the water stood the residence of Gov. Petrus Stuyvesant, his farm, the residences of other personages, and the offices and storehouses of the Dutch West India Company, among others.

ENGLISH NEW YORK, 1739. The English conquered New Netherland in 1664 and achieved permanent ownership of the colony a decade later. This line engraving, drawn by the artist J. Carwithan, shows Fort George as well as the waterside batteries that the British set up to protect the colony from invaders. The mounting of defensive batteries at the waterside gave the area its name, the Battery. Thus when the area was landscaped in 1785, it was logically christened Battery Park.

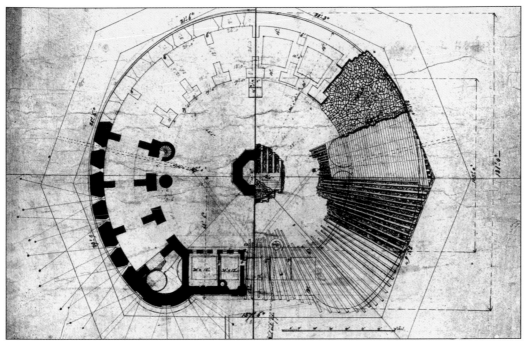

PLANNING A NEW FORTRESS FOR BATTERY PARK. This 1808 drawing shows the original plan of West Battery, later known as Castle Clinton. The initial plans for the new fortress called for it to be constructed on a landfilled isle, which was to be connected to Battery Park by a drawbridge. The military requirements for the fortress were planned and outlined by Col. Jonathan Williams of the Army Corps of Engineers, and the design of the entrance, the getting of construction materials, and other matters were seen to by architect John McComb. (New York City Municipal Archives.)

COL. JONATHAN WILLIAMS. Colonel Williams (1750–1815) is credited with having been the principal force behind the design and planning of West Battery, later known as Castle Clinton, and the East Battery (Castle Williams). A grandnephew of Benjamin Franklin, Colonel Williams was a man of many accomplishments. He was a senior officer in the Army Corps of Engineers and was an expert on fortifications through the study of advanced French military techniques. He also served as the first superintendent of the United States Military Academy at West Point, and before his death, he served as a United States congressman representing his native state, Pennsylvania.

NEW YORK HARBOR AS SEEN FROM THE BATTERY. This artistic work dates from 1811, the year in which the West Battery was completed. The fort stood on a man-made island 200 feet away from the shore. It fired its first salute on Evacuation Day, November 25, 1811. Armed with 28 guns and a garrison of officers and men, the fortification was expected to be of vital importance in securing New York City from foreign attack.

CASTLE CLINTON AND THE BATTERY, 1820. From 1816 to 1820, Castle Clinton served as the headquarters of the Third Military District. In 1815, following the conclusion of the War of 1812, West Battery was renamed Castle Clinton, said to be in honor of DeWitt Clinton, New York City's dynamic mayor. However, after the removal of headquarters to Governors Island, the War Department lost interest in Castle Clinton; it was demilitarized in 1821 and ceded to New York City in March 1822. Two years later, the ex-fort was christened Castle Garden.

Two

Glorious
Castle Garden

General Lafayette's Return, August 16, 1824. This engraving shows the hearty welcome accorded to one of the American Revolution's greatest heroes, the Marquis de Lafayette. His visit was particularly sensational, since he was the only surviving senior military officer still alive. On arrival in New York Harbor, he was taken to Castle Garden. There he changed into his military uniform and entered the city. Earlier that year, city authorities had leased Castle Garden for public entertainment, and it was formally opened on July 3, 1824.

THE MARQUIS DE LAFAYETTE. On September 14, 1824, the Marquis de Lafayette landed at Castle Garden where he was given a grand fete in the presence of 6,000 guests. Marie-Joseph-Paul-Yves-Roch-Gilbert du Motier, marquis de Lafayette, was born at the Chateau de Chavaniac in 1757 and died in Paris in 1834 at the age of 76. A few weeks after his death, a memorial procession was held in which a bronze plaster urn surmounted with the wings of the American eagle was drawn by four white horses into Castle Garden. There Gen. James Tallmadge delivered a heartfelt eulogy to Lafayette.

THE TOUR

OF

LANDING OF GEN. LAFAYETTE.
At Castle Garden, New-York,
16th August, 1824.

GEN. LAFAYETTE.

GENERAL LAFAYETTE'S AMERICAN TOUR. While here, Lafayette toured the United States, where he was received throughout the land with warmth and acclaim.

OPENING THE ERIE CANAL, 1825. This watercolor shows the preparations for cannon fire to help celebrate the opening of the 363-mile Erie Canal on October 26, 1825. DeWitt Clinton (1769–1828), by then governor of New York, was the man most principally responsible for the success attending the canal's construction. The waterway vastly improved transportation and commerce in New York Harbor by connecting the Great Lakes with the Hudson River.

FENCING IN THE BATTERY. In 1826, the city installed this ornamental iron railing around Battery Park at a cost of $25,000. This was one of several repairs to the castle and Battery Park undertaken that year.

THE WATERSIDE RESORT, 1830. Well before this year, Castle Garden's reputation as the city's preferred waterfront resort had already been well established. Crowds of New Yorkers and visitors to the city flocked to Battery Park to listen to concert bands play the most popular airs of the day and watch with excitement displays of fireworks and balloon aeronautics, which were then novelties. Within the castle's walled confines were also permanent exhibits on display such as marble busts and paintings. These two drawings give a notion of the affect Castle Garden had on the manners, customs, and social life of the people of New York

PRESIDENT JACKSON'S ESCAPE, 1833. This engraving shows Pres. Andrew Jackson's near escape from mishap when Castle Garden's drawbridge collapsed just moments after he had ridden over it. The event occurred on June 11, 1833. The picture, drawn in 1857, more than 20 years afterward, quite anachronistically shows Castle Garden roofed over with the rotunda, which was not put up until 1844–1845. (Emerson's United States Magazine, July 1857.)

A BOAT RACE UNDER THE DRAWBRIDGE. This sketch appeared on a cover of a piece of sheet music for the song "Light May the Boat Row," published in 1836. The music was drawn from a popular melody from Northumbria, in the northeast of England, with lyrics by John Watson. Castle Garden's romantic drawbridge attracted many strollers, as well as fishermen and anglers.

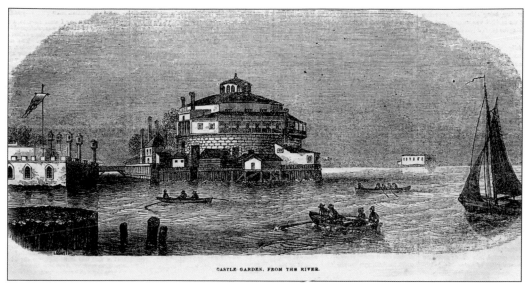

CASTLE GARDEN, FROM THE RIVER.

CASTLE GARDEN'S DOME. In late 1844 and early 1845, Castle Garden was covered over with a magnificent domed rooftop. In this completed form, the circular building had at last achieved classic perfection as a rotunda. This engraving dates from about 1845, the year of its completion.

VISITORS AND IMMIGRANTS, 1847. Artist Samuel Bell Waugh (1814–1885) executed this wonderful painting in 1855. It depicts Castle Garden and the waterfront as it appeared in 1847. Near the castle stands the magnificent Chinese trading junk *Keying*, which thrilled New Yorkers as a glimpse of the romantic East. Meanwhile, at the dockside stands a more commonplace vessel from England bearing a cargo of goods and of immigrants.

THE BATTERY IN 1847

BATTERY PARK, 1847. By this year, the richly treed Battery had achieved a charm ensuring its continual use as a favorite place for strollers. C. J. Cantzler drew this watercolor painting.

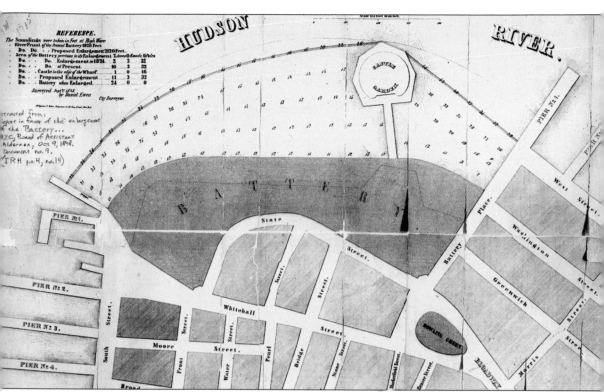

THE ENLARGEMENT OF BATTERY PARK. This drawing from 1848 shows the plan to vastly enlarge Battery Park through landfill operations. As is evident here, the result would end Castle Garden's isolation as a small island only accessible by drawbridge. Instead, the castle would stand on the mainland at the water's edge.

PHINEAS T. BARNUM. In 1850, the legendary showman P. T. Barnum (1810–1891) engaged Sweden's Jenny Lind to sing in America at $1,000 a night for 150 nights, with all expanses paid by Barnum. The tour was an enormous success for both of them. Lind opened her tour with a dazzling performance at Castle Garden.

JENNY LIND, "THE SWEDISH NIGHTINGALE." One of Sweden's greatest opera singers, Lind (1820–1887) had already achieved fame during performances throughout Europe. Her American debut at Castle Garden and subsequent performances throughout the country won her even greater acclaim. She retired from the stage shortly after her return to Europe and settled in the south of England. There she gained popularity as a local philanthropist and professor of singing.

FIRST APPEARANCE OF JENNY LIND IN AMERICA.
At Castle Garden Sept. 11th 1850.
Total Receipts $ 26.238.

THE SWEDISH NIGHTINGALE'S CASTLE GARDEN DEBUT. This engraving depicts Jenny Lind's sensational debut before an audience of 6,000 music lovers at the Castle Garden Theatre on September 11, 1850. The total receipts for her evening's warbling mounted well into the thousands of dollars, quite extraordinary for the period. Among the songs she sang were "Casta Diva," "Per Piacere," and a Norwegian specialty of hers, "Kom Kjyra," known to her English fans as "The Echo Song."

CASTLE GARDEN BY MOONLIGHT. The elegant lithograph shows the famed concert hall as it looked of an evening in the year 1850 around the time of Jenny Lind's performance. The lithograph is in soft colors, mostly shades of blue and green.

PRESIDENT FILLMORE'S VISIT. In May 1851, Pres. Millard Fillmore and members of his cabinet came to New York to take part in the inauguration of the Erie Railroad. The president and cabinet were taken to Castle Garden on the side-wheel ferryboat, the *Erie*. From the castle and Battery Park, the president was escorted to the ceremonies at city hall by mounted troops of the 7th Regiment.

LOLA MONTEZ, DECEMBER 1851. Another European favorite to make her American debut at Castle Garden was the rather notorious exotic dancer Lola Montez (1821–1861). A native of Ireland, Eliza Gilbert recreated herself as "Lola Montez, Spanish Dancer" in 1843. Spectacular fame came quickly when she thrilled Londoners with her "Tarantula Dance" and the expression "Whatever Lola Wants, Lola Gets." In 1846–1848, she was the mistress of Bavaria's eccentric king, Ludwig I, who bestowed upon her the aristocratic titles of Countess Landsfeld and Baroness Rosenthal. The picture shows her one week before she made her debut at Castle Garden.

Louis Kossuth, December 1852. Castle Garden also attracted controversial politicians. Undoubtedly the best known of these was Hungary's overthrown nationalist leader, Lajos "Louis" Kossuth (1802–1894). The eloquent exile gave a speech at Castle Garden such as never had been heard before. He passionately urged the United States to support the independence of Hungary from Austria. Although his harangue drew some American support to his cause, it failed to win a sustained interest.

CASTLE GARDEN AND THE BATTERY, 1852. This scene presents life at the waterfront at Battery Park and likewise gives a first-rate view of the drawbridge to Castle Garden when it was still island-bound.

CASTLE GARDEN'S SALTWATER BATHS, 1853. Seen here is an idyllic view along the Battery's promenade. This picture shows a sign indicating the presence of a saltwater floating bath placed at the side of the drawbridge. The baths were installed around 1825 and remained in place until about 1855. When the castle was joined to Battery Park by landfill, the baths were removed to the newly filled waterside. The salt baths remained until the early years of the 20th century.

CASTLE GARDEN AND THE BATTERY, AROUND 1853. The beautifully landscaped park and inviting promenade of the Battery and Castle Garden continued to cast its spell over visitors from out of town and New Yorkers alike. The presence of swans and deer in an enclosure further added to the park's appeal.

THE AMERICAN INSTITUTE FAIR. In 1853, the 21st American Institute Fair was held at Castle Garden. As can be seen, many of the nation's latest inventions and manufactured items were on exhibit.

CASTLE GARDEN FROM THE BAY. This view from the harbor shows several boats on a rather stormy and blustery day.

BIRD'S-EYE VIEW OF NEW YORK HARBOR. Published in November 1855, this exceptional engraving of New York City and its harbor includes Castle Garden shortly before landfilling operations put an end to its separate existence as an island. On the upper right-hand side is the borough of Brooklyn, which was reached by ferryboats. The bit of land in the lower right-hand side of the picture is Governors Island.

Three

EUROPEAN MASS MIGRATION

EMIGRANT NEEDLEWOMEN ON DECK, 1850. Large numbers of European emigrants began departing in ever-increasing numbers following the end of the Napoleonic wars in 1815. After 1825, even more German, Scandinavian, Irish, French, and Dutch emigrants began joining the British. Subsequent famines in Ireland, Germany, the Low Countries, and Sweden increased the stream. In addition, emigrants set out from northern Italy, Switzerland, Luxembourg, Austria, Hungary, Bohemia, Alsace-Lorraine, and, eventually, from Poland, Russia, Greece, and Portugal.

Nach Amerika für 45 Thlr.

Norddeutscher Lloyd.
Postdampfschiffahrt
von BREMEN nach

137

Newyork	Baltimore	Neworleans
jeden Mittwoch und Sonnabend.	jeden zweiten Dienstag.	24. März. 14. April.
Erste Kajüte 165 Thaler, zweite Kajüte 100 Thaler, Zwischendeck 45 Thaler.	Kajüte 135 Thaler, Zwischendeck 45 Thaler.	Kajüte 210 Thaler, Zwischendeck 55 Thaler.

Nähere Auskunft ertheilen sämmtliche Passagier-Expedienten in Bremen und deren inländische Agenten sowie

Die Direction des Norddeutschen Lloyd.

NORTH GERMAN LLOYD STEAMERS. This advertisement posted by the North German Lloyd Line announces steamship passage available to emigrants desiring to go from Bremen to the American seaports of New York, Baltimore, and New Orleans. Ships of the steamer mail service sailed for New York each Wednesday and each Sunday afternoon. The steerage fare was 45 thalers, while second class cost 100 thalers and first class ran to 145 thalers. As can be seen, ships bound for Baltimore left only once a week, while those sailing to New Orleans left only monthly and were more expensive.

GERMANY'S HAMBURG-AMERIKA LINE. The leading steamship company operating out of the port of Hamburg was the famous Hamburg-Amerika Line. Here the firm offers service to several destinations, with New York being the most prominent. The steerage fare for that destination is quoted at 45 thalers, second class at 100 thalers, and first class at 165 thalers.

36

ENGLAND'S WHITE STAR LINE. The ships of England's White Star Line offered regular steamer service from Liverpool to New York, Boston, and Philadelphia. As can be seen here, steerage fare was £6 and 6 shillings (6 guineas). Children under the age of eight traveled at half fare. The cost included "a plentiful supply of cooked Provisions." It further promised that a surgeon would be available on each vessel and that stewardesses were posted in steerage to attend the women and children. Irish passengers usually boarded the vessels in Queenstown (Cobh), Ireland. (National Park Service.)

THE NETHERLANDS' HOLLAND AMERICA LINE. Based in Rotterdam, the Holland America Line offered weekly steamship service from Rotterdam and Amsterdam directly to New York. The poster shows a Dutch woman and her daughter watching the ships in the harbor. The daughter says, "Where is that ship going to?" and the mother replies, "To America, my child!" The advertisement promises that tickets are available to all points in the United States.

Upon the Deck of a German Ship. Emigrant passengers and some members of the crew are seen here on the steerage deck of a sailing ship, which operated in the early years of the Castle Garden Emigrant Landing Depôt.

A Sailing Vessel. Pictured is a typical sailing ship from the early years of European immigration to the United States.

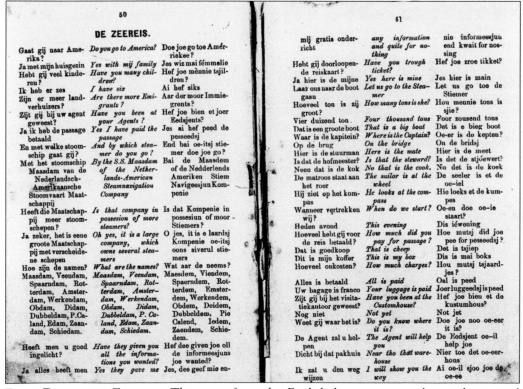

Practische Spraakkunst,

BEKNOPT ZELFONDERRICHT IN DE

ENGELSCHE TAAL.

LEARNING ENGLISH. The Holland-America Line issued a manual on practical English for Dutch emigrants. The volume's subtitle says, "Concise Self-Tuition in the English Tongue."

DE ZEEREIS.

50

Dutch	English	Pronunciation
Gaat gij naar Amerika?	Do you go to America?	Doe joe go toe Amériekee?
Ja met mijn huisgezin	Yes with mij family	Jes wiz mai fémmelie
Hebt gij veel kinderen?	Have you many children?	Hef joe mènnie tsjildren?
Ik heb er zes	I have six	Ai hef siks
Zijn er meer landverhuizers?	Are there more Emigrants?	Aar der moor Immiegrents?
Zijt gij bij uw agent geweest?	Have you been at your Agents?	Hef joe bien et joer Eedsjents?
Ja ik heb de passage betaald	Yes I have paid the passage	Jes ai hef peed de pesseedsj
En met welke stoomschip gaat gij?	And by which steamer do you go?	End bai oe-itsj stiemer doe joe go?
Met het stoomschip Maasdam van de Nederlandsch-Amerikaansche Stoomvaart Maatschappij	By the S.S. Maasdam of the Netherlands-American Steamnavigation Company	Bai de Maasdem of de Nedderlens Ameriken Stiem Navigeesjun Kompenie
Heeft die Maatschappij meer stoomschepen?	Is that company in posession of more steamers?	Is dat Kompenie in possesiun of moor Stiemers?
Ja zeker, het is eene groote Maatschappij met verscheidene schepen	Oh yes, it is a large company, which owns several steamers	O jes, it is e laardsj Kompenie oe-itsj oons siverul stiemers
Hoe zijn de namen?	What are the names?	Wat aar de neems?
Maasdam, Veendam, Spaarndam, Rotterdam, Werkendam, Obdam, Didam, Dubbeldam, P.Caland, Edam, Zaandam, Schiedam.	Maasdam, Veendam, Spaarndam, Rotterdam, Amsterdam, Werkendam, Obdam, Didam, Dubbeldam, P. Caland, Edam, Zaandam, Schiedam.	Maesdem, Viendem, Spaerndem, Rotterdem, Emsterdem, Werkendem, Obdem, Deidem, Dubbeldem, Pie Calend, Iedem, Zaendem, Schiedem.
Heeft men u good ingelicht?	Have they given you all the information you wanted?	Hef dee given joe oll de informeesjuns joe wanted?
Ja alles heeft men	Yes they gave me	Jes, dee geef mie en-

51

Dutch	English	Pronunciation
mij gratis onderricht	any information and quite for nothing	nio informeesjun end kwait for nossing
Hebt gij doorloopende reiskaart?	Have you trough ticket?	Hef joe zroe tikket?
Ja hier is de mijne	Yes here is mine	Jes hier is main
Laat ons naar de boot gaan	Let us go to the Steamer	Let us go toe de Stiemer
Hoeveel ton is zij groot?	How many tons is she?	Hou meunie tons is sjie?
Vier duizend ton	Four thousand tons	Foor zousend tons
Dat is een groote boot	That is a big boat	Det is e bieg boot
Waar is de kapitein?	Where is the Captain?	Oe-er is de kepten?
Op de brug	On the bridge	On de bridsj
Hier is de stuurman	Here is the mate	Hier is de meet
Is dat de hofmeester?	Is that the steward?	Is det de stjoewert?
Neen dat is de kok	No that is the cook.	No det is de koek
De matroos staat aan het roer	The sailor is at the wheel	De seeler is et de oe-iel
Hij ziet op het kompas	He looks at the compass	Hie loeks et de kumpes
Wanneer vertrekken wij?	When do we start?	Oe-en doe oe-ie staart?
Heden avond	This evening	Dis iëwening
Hoeveel hebt gij voor de reis betaald?	How much did you pay for passage?	Hoe mutsj did joe pee for pesseedsj?
Dat is goedkoop	That is cheep	Det is tajiep
Dit is mijn koffer	This is my box	Dis is mai boks
Hoeveel onkosten?	How much charges?	Hou mutsj tajaardjes?
Alles is betaald	All is paid	Oal is peed
Uw bagage is franco	Your luggage is paid	Joer luggeedsj is peed
Zijt gij bij het visitatiekantoor geweest?	Have you been at the Customhouse?	Hef joe bien et de kustumhous?
Nog niet	Not yet	Not jet
Weet gij waar het is?	Do you know where it is?	Doe joe noo oe-eer it is?
De Agent zal u helpen	The Agent will help you	De Eedsjent oe-il help joe
Dicht bij dat pakhuis	Near tho that warehouse	Nier toe det oe-eerhous
Ik zal u den weg wijzen	I will show you the woy	Ai oe-il sjoo joe de oe-ee

FROM DUTCH TO ENGLISH. This page from the English learning manual provides typical phrases regarding the sea voyage in Dutch and translated into English. The third column is the transliteration to help Dutch people pronounce the strange sounds of English. Notice that the Dutch text uses old-fashioned Dutch spellings, such as *gij* for modern *jij* (you).

INTERIOR OF THE EMIGRANT SHIP *SAMUEL HOP*. This engraving of the steerage accommodations of an emigrant ship dates from about the 1850s. (National Park Service.)

EMIGRANTS ON THE STEERAGE DECK. This is another scene from the *Samuel Hop*. (National Park Service.)

MORNING PRAYERS IN STEERAGE. Loss of life was commonplace for travelers crossing the sea, especially in the days of sailing ships. Here passengers pray piously to their God, or, if Catholic or Eastern Orthodox, additional prayers might be made to favorite saints. By the early 1870s, most passenger sailing ships had been replaced by steamers, which traversed the Atlantic much more quickly. (National Park Service.)

Die Schiffsküche.

Morgengebet.

THE SHIP'S COOK. In steerage, food was ladled out of great pots and serving vessels. (National Park Service.)

MAKING MERRY IN STEERAGE. This engraving shows emigrants playing and making merry on the steerage deck of the *Samuel Hop.* (National Park Service.)

SKETCHES OF STEERAGE PASSENGERS. The artist Legamey made this series of "studies from life on the deck of an ocean steamer." (National Park Service.)

ON BOARD THE PENNLAND. Joseph Byron took this photograph of the steerage deck of the SS *Pennland* in 1890. (National Park Service.)

ESPYING THE NEW WORLD—LAND HO! This sketch shows emigrants crowded on board a vessel that is within sight of America. (National Park Service.)

Landungsdepot in Castle-Garden.

CASTLE GARDEN FROM A GERMAN PERIODICAL. The Castle Garden Emigrant Landing Depôt achieved legendary status in Europe as emigrants wrote home about their experiences passing through the facility, and journalists and other writers commented on its operations and wrote human-interest stories about it. (National Park Service.)

Four

THE IMMIGRANT GATEWAY

THE CASTLE GARDEN EMIGRANT LANDING DEPÔT. Castle Garden ceased to be used for theatrical and other public events by 1854–1855. New York State officials, as well as the powerful German and Irish missionary societies, were anxious to use it for immigration purposes, and within months, an agreement to that end was concluded. Shortly afterward, it was transformed into America's first immigrant landing station and opened on August 3, 1855. The New York State Board of Emigration commissioners had charge of the new operation.

GULIAN CROMMELIN VERPLANCK

THE HONORARY GULIAN C. VERPLANCK. The Dutch American politician Gulian C. Verplanck (1786–1870) took a remarkable interest in the many thousands of immigrants arriving in New York each year. In 1847, the former congressman helped to set up the New York State Board of Emigration commissioners and served as its president (1847–1870). Under his leadership, the board opened a refuge for destitute immigrants and a hospital (the Verplanck State Emigrant Hospital) on Ward's Island in 1848 and, seven years later, established the immigrant station inside of old Castle Garden.

THE IMMIGRANT DETENTION BUILDINGS ON WARD'S ISLAND. Located in the East River, Ward's Island consisted of 255 acres. The state emigration commissioners operated several buildings on the island, the most important of which were the Refuge Building for destitute women and children, the New Barracks Building for destitute men, and the hospital. The island was reached by a steamboat, which traveled back and forth between Castle Garden at the Battery and Ward's Island. Additionally, there was a rowing boat service between the 110th Street pier and the island.

46

THE VERPLANCK STATE EMIGRANT HOSPITAL. Named in honor of Gulian C. Verplanck, the hospital on Ward's Island was capable of caring for 350 patients. Since many immigrants were unwell after the sea voyage, the hospital seemed a perfect place for caring for them. At Castle Garden, they were examined by physicians; those found to be suffering from a disease were sent to the Ward's Island Department, whose officers judged whether the immigrant should be hospitalized. The commissioners also operated an isolation hospital for smallpox cases on Blackwell's Island.

STEAMSHIP ROW. These buildings stood roughly where the present United States Customs House stands today. They housed the offices of several steamship lines operating in the port. Such firms included the Anchor Line, the Black Ball Line, the North German Lloyd Line, the French Line (Compagnie Générale Transatlantique), the Cunard Line, and the Red Star Line. The companies' managers and agents were responsible for their piers, the ships (when in port), the cargo, and the passengers and their luggage. The buildings were demolished by the end of the 1890s.

THE IRISH EMIGRANT. This image highlights the arrival of an Irish immigrant named Patrick Murphy. On the right of the image, he can be seen sitting on his box, which reads, "Pat Murfy for Ameriky." The Irish were the second-largest group to immigrate through Castle Garden. One of the founders of the Castle Garden station was a successful immigrant named Andrew Carrigan. Carrigan also founded the Emigrant Savings Bank, which is still in business.

CASTLE GARDEN BAGGAGE LANDING. Immigrants came to New York on sailing ships and transatlantic steamships. After passing quarantine, the ships proceeded into the harbor and dropped anchor near the Battery. Foreign passengers and their luggage were then transferred onto barges, ferries, and steamer tugs, which delivered them to the castle's pier, as seen here. The baggage master's men brought the luggage into the shelter or, in fine weather, left some of it outside.

IMMIGRANTS ARRIVING AT CASTLE GARDEN. Immigrants were brought to Castle Garden's pier on small boats such as the one shown here. New York City police constables assigned to "Castle Garden Duty" helped to keep order and protected foreigners from being molested, swindled, or robbed.

THE OLD IMMIGRATION AT CASTLE GARDEN. Most of Castle Garden's immigrants were Germans, Irish, British, Scandinavians, Swiss, and other western European Protestants and Catholics, especially during the period that spanned the years 1855 through the 1880s. Such immigrants were described as the old immigration. The new immigration, from the 1880s through the 1920s, primarily constituted Italians, Slavs, Jews, and Greeks.

THE NEW IMMIGRANTS AT CASTLE GARDEN. The 1880s saw a decided rise in the number of immigrants coming from southern and eastern Europe. This engraving shows how some of them looked when they arrived at Castle Garden. Many of them hailed from southern Italy, the Russian Empire, Austria-Hungary, Greece, Romania, and the Ottoman Empire.

DAS MUSS DER PALAST SEIN. The magnificent sight of Castle Garden and its domed roof dazzled many newcomers, particularly peasants and villagers from the poorer regions of Europe. These Germans gaze in awe at the castle, while the father, thinking in terms familiar to him from his socially hierarchical homeland, mutters, "That must be the palace." The engraving dates from about 1870. (Harper's Magazine.)

SHELTER. Here is a scene of immigrants waiting by the heavy stone walls of Castle Garden.

IN CONFERENCE. Immigrants gathered to discuss their problems as well as the situation at hand and how best to proceed.

IN THE LAND OF PROMISE—CASTLE GARDEN, 1884. This painting, and the two that follow, captures the patience that immigrants needed as they waited to be registered in Castle Garden. The artist is Charles F. Ulrich (1858–1908.)

IMMIGRANT TYPES. Clearly these immigrants are from northern or western Europe, the region that sent the greatest number through the station.

THE PENSIVE CHILD. Holding an umbrella, a vessel for pouring liquids, and a piece of fruit, the youngster is stilled by the strange scene, the babbling voices, the curious odors, and the variety of folk costumes worn by peoples of so many different nationalities.

Innere Ansicht des Landungsdepots in Castle-Garden.

WITHIN THE WALLS OF CASTLE GARDEN. This engraving was published in a German periodical.

MORMONS AT CASTLE GARDEN, 1880S. The Church of Jesus Christ of Latter-day Saints brought over foreigners who had converted to the Mormon religion. Many came from northern Germany, Denmark, Sweden, Finland, and other Protestant sections of Europe. Youthful Mormon elders escorted the women and families to Utah and other places for settlement.

MORMON EMIGRANTS AT CASTLE GARDEN, NEW YORK.

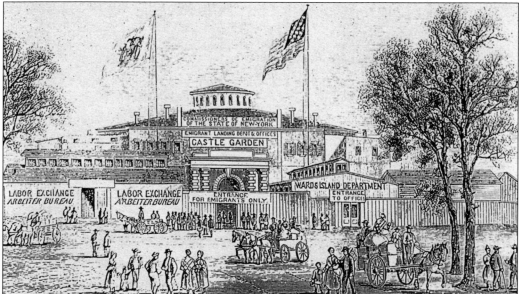

THE CASTLE GARDEN COMPLEX. This view of the immigrant station from the park shows the location of some of its offices. To the left, the labor exchange served immigrants seeking work by allowing prospective employers a chance to advertise available situations either through the notice board or by posting an agent inside. The Ward's Island Department, to the right, was in charge of detaining aliens who were either destitute or ill. Those whom the department detained were then sent to Ward's Island.

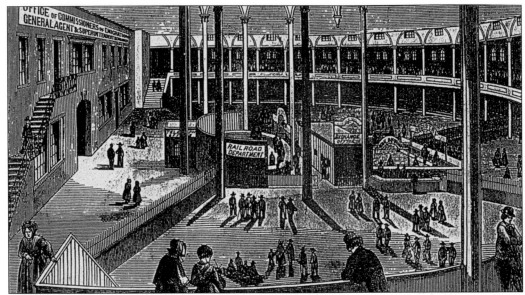

CASTLE GARDEN'S DEPARTMENTS. This drawing shows the disposition of the bureaucratic offices inside of the castle. Newly arrived aliens entered on the right, after having submitted to a quick medical examination. After a brief spell in a waiting room, they pressed forward to the registry, where clerks recorded their names and personal details. After having completed this step, they could go forward to the exchange office to change their money into American currency. Next came the Railroad Department, where tickets could be purchased, and a telegraph office to send cables. To the left is the main door leading to Battery Park. The stairs above it led to the offices of the superintendent, the treasurer, and other officials.

IN THE WAITING ROOM. Here immigrants could relax a bit after having left the barge that had brought them from their transatlantic ship. The long voyage could be a wearisome affair.

THE REGISTRY DEPARTMENT. This department's clerks, divided into English and foreign language sections, interviewed the newcomers, recording their names, nationalities, old residences, and destinations. They also occasionally checked to ensure that immigrants who seemed vulnerable had enough money with them to survive in the new country until work could be found. After registering was completed, immigrants were directed to the Railroad, Telegraph, Information, Forwarding, or Letter-Writing Departments.

REGISTERING AN ALIEN. This close-up scene at the Registry Department shows a clerk interviewing an immigrant woman.

THE MONEY EXCHANGE BROKERS. Immigrants usually exchanged coins of gold, silver, copper, or nickel in exchange for United States coinage and paper currency. The exchange brokers received a commission for their work.

EXCHANGE BROKER'S OFFICE. *HM Mar 1871*

A CLOSE-UP OF THE MONEY EXCHANGE. The brokers changed to dollars and cents such foreign money as British pounds, crowns, and shillings, German thalers and marks, French francs, Swedish riksdalers and kronor, Austrian guldens, thalers, and ducats, Dutch guilders, Belgian francs, Italian centesimi and lire, Russian rubles, Greek drachmas, Portuguese reis and coroas, Swiss francs, and Spanish reales and pesetas. Immigrants were sometimes cheated, receiving less in United States currency than they were due.

A REUNION OF FRIENDS. As one might expect, the reuniting of relations, friends, and acquaintances was a common experience at Castle Garden.

DISTRIBUTING TRACTS. Protestant missionaries, such as Methodists, Baptists, and Presbyterians, handed out Christian tracts to interested foreigners and foisted a plentiful number on those quite uninterested as well. The texts of these tracts were written in several languages, including German, Dutch, Swedish, Danish, Finnish, and French, as well as in English.

THE LABOR BULLETIN. Job announcements were posted daily upon the labor exchange's bulletin board. Employers eagerly sought household servants, cabinetmakers, tailors, shoemakers, bakers, brewers, weavers, gardeners, and common laborers.

HIRING SERVANTS. All manner of servants were in great demand. In fact, this kind of occupation was the main avenue for immigrant women and girls to find respectable work and to attain a degree of independence from their families, if they wished. Germans, Irishwomen, Englishwomen, Scotswomen, Swedes, Danes, Norwegians, Dutchwomen, and Swiss often sought this kind of post. They often worked as cooks, maids, dressmakers, shop assistants, or charwomen in private homes, hotels, hospitals, shops, and offices. Men took positions as gardeners, coachmen, butlers, footmen, valets, waiters, mechanics, janitors, and sextons.

LABOR EXCHANGE. Although the welcoming of prospective employers and their representatives into Castle Garden was a help in finding immediate work for newcomers, it was likewise an invitation to dishonest persons on the watch for greenhorns to exploit, defraud, rob, or swindle.

SWINDLERS AT THE LABOR EXCHANGE. Here sharpers try to swindle immigrants. Indeed, one of them, on the left, is looking for valuables in someone's bag. (National Park Service.)

NORSE NEWCOMERS. These three women and five children from Norway were sketched outside the walls of Castle Garden. Norwegians began immigrating to the United States in 1825. Thousands and thousands more followed these first settlers. Seemingly hopeless poverty and hardship, as well as unhappiness over the social structure and Swedish rule over their native land made America tremendously inviting. The Norwegians settled throughout the Northeast, the Midwest, and the West; most of them were homesteaders.

THE ERIE FERRY, 1868. Ferries, such as the one sketched here, transferred immigrants from Castle Garden to the Erie Railway depot across the Hudson River. From there, travelers might continue their journey to places as far away as Ohio, Kentucky, Illinois, Michigan, Missouri, and California.

CASTLE GARDEN POSTCARD. Although the clerks of the Letter-Writing Department usually wrote to notify friends and relations of an immigrant's arrival, missionaries also obliged. An example of this is pictured above in the form of a postcard written at Castle Garden on October 22, 1884. The recipient, Fredrick Johansson Rodeen (1849–1911), was from Lavsocken, Vastergotland, Sweden, and had immigrated through Castle Garden in August 1884. His wife, Sarah, came that October with their four children. In 1888 or 1889, Fredrick filed homestead papers in Pillager, Minnesota.

THE MESSAGE OF THE POSTCARD. Written by Norwegian Lutheran missionary P. Peterson in Norwegian intermixed with Swedish, it reads, "Castle Garden, the 22 October 1884. Mr. F. Rodeed, I wish to let you know that your family has to-day, this 22nd of October, landed here at Castle Garden. They appear to be healthy but without either food or money. But don't be concerned. I shall see that they have all they need—I shall pack their suitcases so as to get them ready for their journey. They are leaving from here to-day. P. Peterson, Emigrant Missionary, Castle Garden, New York." The postcard was addressed to Mr. F. Rodeen, Cokato, Wright County, Minnesota. (Provided and translated by Verlyn D. Anderson, Ph.D.)

BLAUVELT'S CASTLE GARDEN. The artist Charles F. Blauvelt drew this marvelous picture to highlight Castle Garden as the gateway to German immigrants. The appearance of the imperial German flag and the United States flag underlines the pride that Germans living abroad felt about the unification of their native land as a single empire under Prussian leadership following the Franco-Prussian War of 1871.

LOOKING FOR RECRUITS, 1861. At the time of the Civil War, both Union and Confederate armies benefited by signing up immigrants as fighting men. The extent to which the United States Army aggressively sought foreign manpower was underlined when it set up a recruiting camp at the Battery, adjacent to the immigrant depot. Notable immigrants who served the Union during that war included Michael (Mike) Corcoran from Ireland, Franz Siegel from Germany, and Joseph Pulitzer from Hungary. In August 1862, the heroic General Corcoran of the Fighting 69th Regiment was acclaimed at Castle Garden by Mayor George Opdyke.

THE FIGHTING 69TH REGIMENT. The popularity of the Union's heroic Irish American regiment continued after the end of the Civil War, as is attested by this sheet music cover published in 1875. Castle Garden, Castle Williams, and the Battery appear on the cover art. The song was a hit in music halls, saloons, and family parlors. Sung by the legendary Tony Hart and the Cadet Corps, it was composed by Dave Braham, and the lyrics were written by Hart's equally celebrated partner, Edward Harrigan.

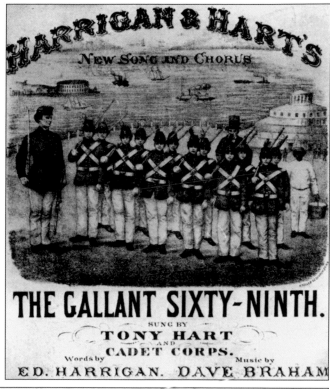

CASTLE GARDEN, 1866. Photographer E. H. Anthony shot this early picture of the immigrant station. (New York Public Library.)

TAKING THE AIR. In this photograph, also from 1866, 10 men are pictured taking their ease in the Battery. (New York Public Library.)

VIEW OF THE IMMIGRANT STATION AND THE BATTERY, 1868. Several buildings standing outside of the castle proper supported the operations of the immigrant station. Of these, the labor exchange, the Ward's Island Department, and the infirmary are particularly prominent. (National Park Service.)

THE LANDFILL OPERATIONS AT THE BATTERY, 1869. The project to enlarge the Battery went on for years, and critics could not help but note that the project reeked with graft and crookedness. The landfilling operations went on from around 1853 to 1872.

SMALL-POX AT CASTLE GARDEN.

Yesterday afternoon, George Murray, one of the crew on board the steam-ship Columbia, from Glasgow, was conveyed to Castle Garden, suffering from small pox. Dr. Sterling had the sufferer taken at once to Blackwell's Island Hospital. The day before, two cases were found on board the France, from Liverpool, Christina Voepel and her husband, from Germany. They were also taken to Blackwell's Island, and their eight children were taken in charge by the Emigration Commissioner and sent to Ward's Island. Yesterday Commissioners Starr and Lynch, of the Castle Garden Committee, visited the Landing Bureau and made inquiries as to the arrangements that existed for landing persons suffering from contagious diseases. Col. Coonan and Dr. Sterling conducted the Commissioners over the department and through the hospital at Castle Garden,

SMALLPOX SCARE AT CASTLE GARDEN, 1873. Contagious diseases were nearly impossible to control prior to the 20th century. The immigrant described in this newspaper story was removed from Castle Garden and sent to the smallpox hospital on Blackwell's Island. (New York Times.)

IMMIGRANT AID SOCIETIES. Although numerous immigrant aid societies sent Christian missionaries and other representatives to Castle Garden, only two organizations had seats on the board of emigration commissioners. These were the powerful German and Irish immigrant aid societies, which were led by the likes of Irish American banker Andrew Carrigan (1805–1872) and German American lawyer and author Friedrich Kapp (1824–1884), both prominent figures of the time. In 1874, however, the societies dedicated to immigrants from France, German-controlled Alsace-Lorraine (Elsaß-Lothringen), Sweden, Scandinavia, and Italy unsuccessfully pleaded for seats on the board. (New York Times.)

THE CASTLE GARDEN FIRE OF 1876. On July 9, 1876, just days after America's centennial celebrations, the immigrant station was partially destroyed in a dreadful fire. Much of the interior was burned completely or damaged by smoke and water. Beside the castle's fire resistant stone walls, only the labor exchange, the infirmary, and the Intelligence Office survived. The cost of the fire was initially estimated at $35,000. (New York Times.)

CASTLE GARDEN IN FLAMES. Ranger Dave McCutcheon recently painted this vivid picture showing the heroic efforts of the Fire Department of the City of New York (FDNY) in bringing one of the city's most terrific fires under control. (Dave McCutcheon, 2006.)

FROM THE WATERFRONT. The newly constructed station was distinguished by an altogether different design for the castle's cupola. This picture dates from about 1877.

UPPER VIEW OF THE CASTLE, 1878. The castle remained one of the city's most distinctive waterside structures.

LOOKING TOWARD THE BATTERY, 1878. On view here is a typical scene from underneath the elevated railway. (New York Public Library.)

TREES IN LEAF. By the 1870s, the park had become decidedly less alluring than it had been in the days of the Castle Garden Theatre. (New York Public Library.)

ARAB REFUGEES. This newspaper article concerns the dramatic escape some Tunisians made from a military prison in Cayenne, French Guiana. Their arrival at Castle Garden is one of the earliest reported instances of Arab refugees landing in America. (New York Times.)

View of the State Emigrant Landing Depot, Castle Garden, N. Y., from the Land Side.
With Governor's Island and Castle William, and Bedloe's Island in the distance.

A GLIMPSE OF THE HARBOR, 1867. Here is a good view of the Emigrant Landing Depôt and the harbor's two fortified islands, Governors Island and Bedloe's Island.

VIEW OF THE ELEVATED RAILWAY AND THE BATTERY, 1885. This live sketch of the elevated railway at South Ferry and the Battery shows Castle Garden in the distance.

CASTLE GARDEN. Done in oils, this painting of the station also shows immigrants on the walkway, boats, and dock.

NEW YORK HARBOR FROM THE WASHINGTON BUILDING, 1887. Built in 1883, the Washington Building stood just across from the Battery. Its upper floors served as convenient vantage points for photographers wishing to get a panoramic shot of the area. In view are the steamboat landing, the Battery, Castle Garden, the elevated railway with a train on it, and harbor boats, while the recently unveiled statue of "Liberty Enlightening the World," an import from Paris, looms in the distance in its new home on Bedloe's Island. (New York Public Library.)

CASTLE GARDEN AND BAY, AROUND 1888. At this period, Castle Garden's reputation had slid considerably due to many scandals, including deceptive practices such as cheating immigrants out of their money, poor sanitation, and other violations of state policies. (National Park Service.)

NEW YORK.—WELCOME TO THE LAND OF FREEDOM—AN OCEAN STEAMER PASSING THE STATUE OF LIBERTY: SCENE ON THE STEERAGE DECK.

WELCOME TO THE LAND OF FREEDOM. The recent addition to the harbor of France's great gift to America, the Statue of Liberty, gave immigrants an even greater hope of their future in America. This scene is on a steerage deck. (Frank Leslie's Illustrated Newspaper.)

TO INVESTIGATE BIGLIN.

ALLEGED EXCESSIVE BAGGAGE CHARGES AT CASTLE GARDEN.

The main energies of yesterday's session of the Emigration Board were devoted to an attempt to prove that the Castle Garden Express Company, the institution which is under the management of Bernard Biglin, has been overcharging emigrants for handling their baggage. Biglin has a contract with the commission by which he is allowed to have a stand at the Garden and to handle such baggage as is not specially ordered to be taken care of by other express companies. This privilege amounts practically to a monopoly of the Castle Garden baggage express. The rates are, however, regulated by the Commissioners.

According to an affidavit placed in the hands of the Commissioners by Adolph Immergist, a passenger who arrived Monday on the Fulda, one of Biglin's men, Fritz Ritterhaus, made Immergist pay 25 cents apiece for the "storage" of eight pieces of baggage from Monday night until Wednesday morning. It seems that the emigrant came to the Garden with an expressman whom he had hired outside, and was charged $2 by Ritterhaus for taking the baggage from the room in Castle Garden to the gates. Biglin denied that anything had been charged for storage, and said that the emigrant had asked the delivery to his own man, and had been perfectly willing to pay the $2 in order to hasten the operation.

In the opinion of President Ridgway this charge was unjust, and it was voted to appoint a committee of three to investigate the entire matter of the handling of emigrants' baggage. Commissioners Wylie, Ulrich, and Stephenson were put on this committee. It is very probable that their researches will result in a radical change at the Garden, as one of the Commissioners said openly yesterday that the present arrangement put Biglin in a position where it would be a very easy thing to impose upon the emigrants.

INVESTIGATIONS AT CASTLE GARDEN. Matters were growing more and more serious at Castle Garden toward the end of the 1880s. This press report covers one of several investigations that were proceeded with at the station. In this case, Bernard Biglin and his Castle Garden Express Company were accused of overcharging immigrants for deliveries. The firm held the exclusive monopoly of delivering immigrants' baggage to addresses in the city. Biglin continued these practices years later, when he briefly held a similar concession at Ellis Island. (New York Times.)

Five

SETTLERS AND HOMESTEADERS

LABOR AND LIFE. Most immigrants to America joined the laboring class, for they did not have the means of setting up shops and businesses of their own. The wide range of employment available included work in factories, mills, shops, and construction sites. Above is a scene of kitchen workers washing up dishes and cutlery at the posh Hotel Astor in New York City. The year was 1904.

IRISH CLAM DIGGERS. Each ethnic group tended to follow certain lines of work. An instance of this is seen in this photograph from 1882. This picture is of Irish immigrants working as clam diggers in Boston, an occupation that at the time was filled with Irish people. The Irish also were mill workers, dockworkers, ditch diggers, and commission agents. Among other nationalities, Germans could be found working as merchants, engineers, or musicians; the Swedes very often were carpenters, lumberjacks, and farmers; and the French and Spanish Basques nearly always went to Nevada to work as shepherds.

HISTORIC ST. BRIGID'S CHURCH. Hundreds of thousands of Irish Catholics entered the United States, fleeing the potato blight that had caused famine and disease in their beloved homeland. Driven by their strong Roman Catholic faith, they constructed churches to their most powerful saints. Built in 1848, St. Brigid's Church in New York's Lower East Side was one of the very first churches built by and for the famine immigrants. (Painted by Dave McCutcheon, 2005.)

UNION PACIFIC, 1888. The advertisement in French was published in Canada and encouraged immigrants to book passage for Kansas and Nebraska.

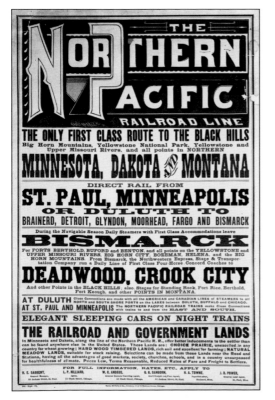

NORTHERN PACIFIC, 1872. Here would-be homesteaders were urged to seek lands along the railway line of the Northern Pacific. The areas advertised were Minnesota, Dakota Territory, and Montana Territory. German, British, Scandinavian, Czech, Dutch, Belgian, and Irish immigrants joined Americans in settling in this region.

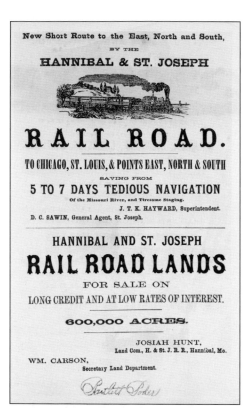

New Short Route to the East, North and South,
BY THE
HANNIBAL & ST. JOSEPH

RAIL ROAD.

TO CHICAGO, ST. LOUIS, & POINTS EAST, NORTH & SOUTH

SAVING FROM

5 TO 7 DAYS TEDIOUS NAVIGATION

Of the Missouri River, and Tiresome Staging.

J. T. K. HAYWARD, Superintendent.

D. C. SAWIN, General Agent, St. Joseph.

HANNIBAL AND ST. JOSEPH

RAIL ROAD LANDS

FOR SALE ON

LONG CREDIT AND AT LOW RATES OF INTEREST.

600,000 ACRES.

JOSIAH HUNT,
Land Com., H. & St. J. R. R., Hannibal, Mo.

WM. CARSON,
Secretary Land Department.

THE HANNIBAL AND ST. JOSEPH RAILROAD.
Missouri was a very attractive place of settlement for the Germans, British, Dutch, and others in the 1860s. Many immigrants arrived by rail from New York, while others entered by way of the port of New Orleans and took riverboats up the Mississippi to reach their destination in Missouri and other regions.

INSIDE A "MODERN SHIP OF THE PLAINS." Trains crossing the vast regions of America were likened to the ships traversing the seas. This sort of railway carriage accommodated family parties to the Great Plains. The picture was drawn in 1885. (Harper's Weekly.)

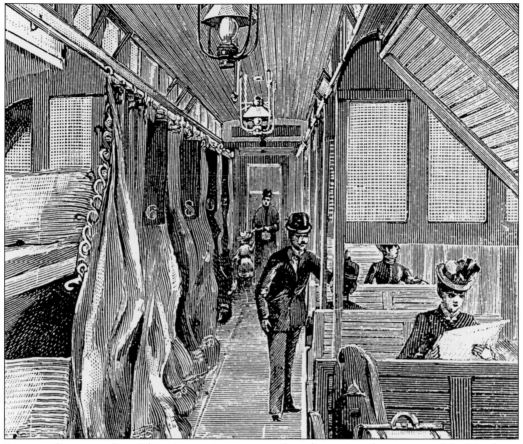

INSIDE A SLEEPING CAR. This picture gives a sense of conditions in a sleeping car of the Northern Pacific Railroad. It dates from April 1889.

AN EMIGRANT TRAIN OF "PENNSYLVANIA" WAGONS

EMIGRANT WAGON TRAIN. Here is a train of Pennsylvania wagons carrying immigrants.

A CHARACTER SCENE IN THE EMIGRANT WAITING-ROOM OF THE UNION PACIFIC RAILROAD DEPOT AT OMAHA.

THE OMAHA RAILWAY DEPOT, 1877. The Union Pacific Railroad set up special waiting rooms for immigrants at many of its railway stations. This character scene shows the Union Pacific's depot at Omaha. Note the admonition for "Black Hillers" to take notice that luncheon baskets could be filled for the price of a quarter.

A TOWN IN THE WEST. A crowd of people, wagons, and horses in the American West is seen in this image.

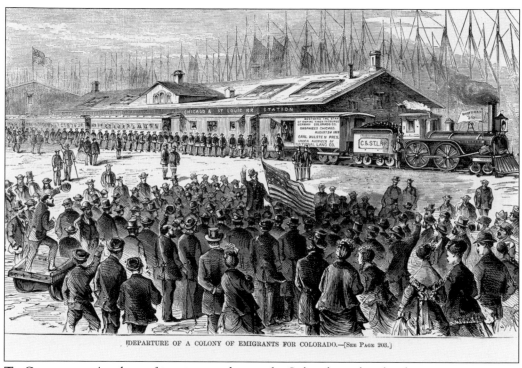

DEPARTURE OF A COLONY OF EMIGRANTS FOR COLORADO.—[SEE PAGE 203.]

TO COLORADO. A colony of immigrants departs for Colorado in this sketch.

LOCOMOTIVE NO. 120. Seen here is an emigrant train around 1869.

A ZULU TRAIN. Zulu trains transported large parties of immigrants, particularly families, to the West. This one, which was also loaded with household goods, livestock, and pets, halted at Mill City, Nevada, in 1886.

THE OVERLAND TRAIL. In 1882, F. M. Baker made this photographic exposure on the flats between Elk Mountain and Mill Creek on the Overland Trail.

MONTANA OR BUST. This party of immigrants with cattle and wagon was photographed at Anaconda, Montana Territory, in the year 1865. (Library of Congress.)

AN IMMIGRANT SETTLEMENT IN MISSOURI. The caption for this idealistic picture reads, "We left our beloved country to be happy and free in the country of the free."

A SOD HOUSE. Vast regions of the northern plains were timberless, and in order to survive the cold winters, homesteaders had little choice but to build their homes out of sod, the grassy topsoil of the surrounding country. (National Park Service.)

A SOD HOUSE IN SOUTH DAKOTA. Scandinavian immigrant H. A. Fadness built this house of sod. It measured 14 feet by 16 feet, and the walls were 3 feet thick. This picture was taken in 1890. (National Park Service.)

A Log Cabin at Swede Lake, 1896. Built in 1856, this log cabin stood at Swede Lake, Minnesota. At the time the photograph was taken, it was the home of Daniel Justus.

Six

CASTLE GARDEN'S LEGACY

AT THE BARGE OFFICE DOCK. A crowd of newly arrived European immigrants with their luggage is seen at the Barge Office dock in 1890. The Barge Office stood near Castle Garden.

THE LANDING AT THE BATTERY. Here is another common scene of immigrants and wagons at the Battery.

CASTLE GARDEN CLERKS, 1890. The staff at Castle Garden was large and included registry clerks, translators, physicians, guards, and baggage handlers. This picture of several clerks of the Registry Department was taken at the Barge Office. Following Castle Garden's closing in 1890, these badged men were hired by the new United States Bureau of Immigration to work as inspectors at Ellis Island. Pictured are, from left to right, (first row) Najeeb J. Arbeely, M. N. Gilbertson, D. T. van Duzer, and R. W. Conradson; (second row) Christian A. Raven, Sven A. Smith, and Charles Semsey. (National Park Service.)

CASTLE GARDEN CLOSED. Here the former Emigrant Landing Depôt has a decidedly abandoned air. This picture was taken in 1892, the year in which Ellis Island opened as its successor. Although immigrant processing had ended at Castle Garden, the German and Irish immigrant aid societies temporarily continued running the labor exchange inside the building.

ALMA E. MATHEWS, PROTESTANT MISSIONARY. Alma E. Mathews (1867–1933) spent her life as a missionary for the Methodist Church. In 1889, she came to New York to work at the church's newly opened Immigrant Girls' Home across the street from Castle Garden. She aided Protestant immigrant women and girls at Castle Garden and, after it closed, continued her work at Ellis Island. At her retirement party in June 1928, to her surprise, the kindly Christian lady was given $1,500 in gold and was proclaimed the "Mother of Aliens."

THE MISSION OF OUR LADY OF THE ROSARY AND THE LEO HOUSE. Artist Dave McCutcheon painted this scene of two Roman Catholic missions in State Street, directly across the road from Castle Garden and Battery Park. Our Lady of the Rosary (1883–1954) served Irish Catholics, and the Leo House (1888–1920) served German Catholics. Nearby were St. Joseph's Society for Polish Immigrants and the Methodist Church's Immigrant Girls' Home. Our Lady of the Rosary is the only one still standing and now houses the shrine to Mother Seton.

THE BARGE OFFICE, 1884. A waterfront view of the newly built Barge Office is shown. The structure was completed for the U.S. Department of the Treasury in 1883. It provided office space for the Customs Service, the Bureau of Immigration (1890–1911), and the Marine Hospital Service (1892–1911). It was demolished in 1911.

BARGE OFFICE CLOSE-UP. The Barge Office supported the Ellis Island operation until it was demolished in 1911.

JANE NOONAN, THE OLD APPLE WOMAN. Irish immigrant Jane Noonan was already 70 years old when she was photographed sitting at the side of her fruit stand in 1900. Noonan emigrated through Castle Garden from County Kerry and sold apples inside of the depot for years. After Ellis Island replaced the castle, she moved her trade to the entrance gate of the Ellis Island ferry at the Barge Office. She lived in nearby Washington Street and probably bought her supply of fruit and other items at the huge Washington Market. Noonan remained a daily figure at the Ellis Island ferry landing until 1906.

SUNSET AT CASTLE GARDEN. This painting shows Castle Garden in April 1890, at the end of its days as an immigrant landing station. In the foreground is Jane Noonan, the old Irish apple woman. (Dave McCutcheon, 2006.)

ENGLISH SINGING GIRLS, 1890. Taken at the Barge Office, these English immigrants were the same type who would have been seen at Castle Garden and later at Ellis Island.

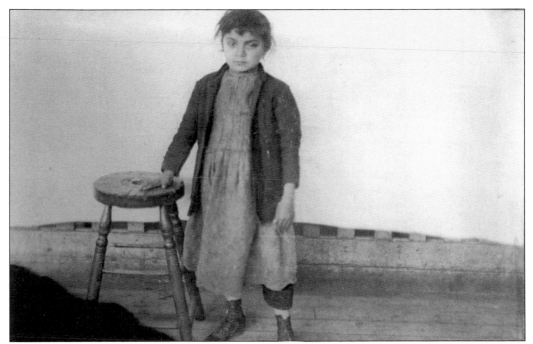

A SYRIAN GIRL, 1890. Bahyeh Brook, age three, was photographed at the Barge Office. She probably came from the region of Syria called Lebanon. At the time, the whole region and its peoples still owed allegiance to the Turkish sultan.

GERMANS FROM RUSSIA, 1890. During this period, large numbers of Germans left their farms in Russia behind, opting for a future in North America. North Dakota was a favorite settlement area for many of them.

SWISS PEASANTS, 1890. Thousands of Swiss immigrants came to America in the 19th century. Most traveled by rail to the northern French seaports of Le Havre and Cherbourg.

A DUTCH FAMILY, 1890. A great many Dutch immigrants, particularly Protestant Christians, came to America during this period. Many settled in Michigan, Missouri, and other parts of the Midwest.

DETAINED ITALIANS, 1890. Southern Italians such as these caused quite a stir when they began leaving their ancient land. Many Americans wondered if they could really assimilate into the dominant Protestant Anglo-Saxon society.

AN AUSTRIAN IMMIGRANT, 1890. Austria sent a large number of immigrants to the United States, particularly after the Civil War.

SCOTCH BOYS, 1890. Taken at the Barge Office dock, these Scottish lads should easily have fit into the mainstream of American life, as they would have spoken fluent English (but with a Scottish brogue), would almost certainly have been Protestant, and were from Great Britain, America's mother country.

A LARGE DUTCH FAMILY, 1890. This family of 11 immigrants from Holland was also photographed at the Barge Office dock.

DUTCH IMMIGRANTS IN CLOGS, 1890. The Dutch brought many of their unique customs to the United States, including their costumes, cookery, language, religion, and values.

A DUTCHMAN AND HIS FAMILY, 1890. This family of three from the Netherlands was also photographed at the Barge Office dock.

ELLIS ISLAND IN 1892. This painting by Dave McCutcheon shows the original Main Building, which was a pinewood structure. Thousands of immigrants passed through it, including future famous Americans such as sportsman Knute Rockne and novelist Ole Rolvaag from Norway, poet Kahlil Gibran from Syria, priest Francis Hodur from Poland, and Broadway star Al Jolson from Russia. In June 1897, the building was destroyed in an intense fire. A new Main Building, one made of bricks, steel, and limestone, was soon constructed and opened in December 1900.

JOSEPH PULITZER. The noted newspaper publisher Joseph Pulitzer (1847–1911) immigrated through Castle Garden in 1864 and quickly signed on as a soldier in the Union army. Afterward, the Hungarian immigrant settled in St. Louis and went into the newspaper business, eventually founding the *St. Louis Post-Dispatch*. In 1883, he took over the *New York World* and made it a competitive daily paper. In 1904, he established the Pulitzer Prize and endowed Columbia University's school of journalism.

JAMES J. DAVIS. Welsh immigrant James John Davies (1873–1947) passed through Castle Garden in 1881. His family settled in Pennsylvania, and he grew up and became an iron puddler. Eventually he rose to prominence in his trade union and became a figure of national importance. He served as secretary of labor (1921–1930) under three presidents and ended his career as a United States senator.

NIKOLA TESLA. The great scientific genius Nikola Tesla (1856–1943) came from Croatia and passed through Castle Garden in 1884. After working for Thomas Edison and George Westinghouse, Tesla set up his own laboratory. His most noted inventions include the Tesla coil, which contributed in a major way to the development of modern broadcasting. Near the end of his life, Tesla worked on a mysterious weapon called the death ray, which interested both the United States and German governments.

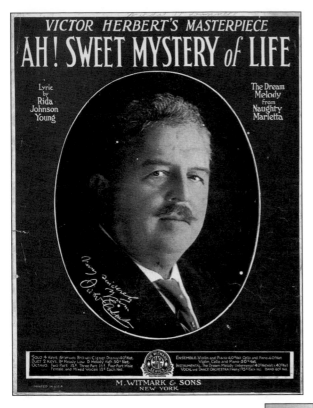

VICTOR HERBERT. This Irish immigrant composed some of America's most beloved operettas. Landing at Castle Garden in 1886, Victor Herbert (1859–1924) and his wife became active in New York's world of classical music. However, he excelled at writing operettas and soon composed the immensely popular *Babes in Toyland* (1903), *Mlle. Modiste* (1905), *The Red Mill* (1906), and *Naughty Marietta*. The songs for which he is best remembered include "Ah! Sweet Mystery of Life," "Kiss Me Again," and "I'm Falling in Love with Someone."

SOPHIE TUCKER. This legendary vaudevillian, singer, and show business personality emigrated from Russia and passed through Castle Garden as an infant. Sophie Tucker (1884–1966) made her name in ragtime and entertained vaudeville and nightclub audiences for years. She was a popular recording artist, especially in the Roaring Twenties. Her hit songs include "Some of These Days," "After You've Gone," and "There'll Be Some Changes Made." She also had a hit with the sentimental favorite "My Yiddische Mama."

LOUIS WOLFE GILBERT. Born in Odessa, Russia, this future composer of American popular music came to America when very young. L. Wolfe Gilbert (1886–1971) wrote such Tin Pan Alley hits as "Waiting for the Robert E. Lee" (1912), "Down Yonder" (1921), "Ramona" (1927), "The Peanut Vendor" (1931), and "Marta" (1931). "Ramona" and "Marta" were million-selling hit records for pop singers Gene Austin and Arthur Tracy.

CHARLES P. STEINMETZ. Germany's scientific genius Charles Proteus Steinmetz (1865–1923) immigrated through Castle Garden in June 1889. Later in life, he recalled his immigration, saying, "When I landed at Castle Garden from the steerage of a French liner I had ten dollars and no job and could speak no English." The electrical engineer and mathematician discovered magnetic hysteresis, a simple notation for calculating alternating current circuits and lighting arresters for high-power transmission lines. For his revolutionary work at the General Electric Company he was proclaimed the "Wizard of G.E."

Saint Frances Xavier Cabrini

MOTHER CABRINI. In 1889, Pope Leo XIII sent Maria Francesca Xavier Cabrini (1850–1917) to America to help Italian immigrants in distress. Passing through Castle Garden with five nuns, Mother Cabrini proved to be one of the greatest helpers of the poor that the nation had ever seen. She founded orphanages, schools, and hospitals for Roman Catholics throughout the country.

ST. FRANCES XAVIER CABRINI. Following her death in Chicago, miracles began to be attributed to the late mother superior and foundress of the Missionary Sisters of the Sacred Heart. In 1946, she became the first American citizen to be canonized a Christian saint. Catholic immigrants are particularly devoted to her.

Seven

THE NEW YORK AQUARIUM

THE NEW YORK AQUARIUM, 1899. On December 10, 1896, the New York Aquarium was opened inside of Castle Garden, giving the old structure a new purpose. The aquarium's first director was the noted zoologist Dr. Tarleton H. Bean (1846–1916). Although he initially set the new institution along professional lines, municipal politics intervened, and Bean was forced out of the position in 1899. The picture above was taken during the celebratory festivities for Adm. George Dewey's naval victory in the Philippines during the Spanish-American War. (New York Public Library)

CASTLE GARDEN AND BATTERY PARK, AROUND 1900. The presence of the New York Aquarium at Castle Garden encouraged the city to improve conditions at the Battery. (New York Public Library.)

VIEW OF THE BATTERY, 1898. At the time, the prominent structures at the Battery included the aquarium, the Washington Building, the Christian mission homes for immigrants, the elevated railway, and the ferryboat terminals.

THE BATTERY AND HARBOR, 1898. In the distance lies Ellis Island, which was at the time briefly closed for reconstruction after a fire.

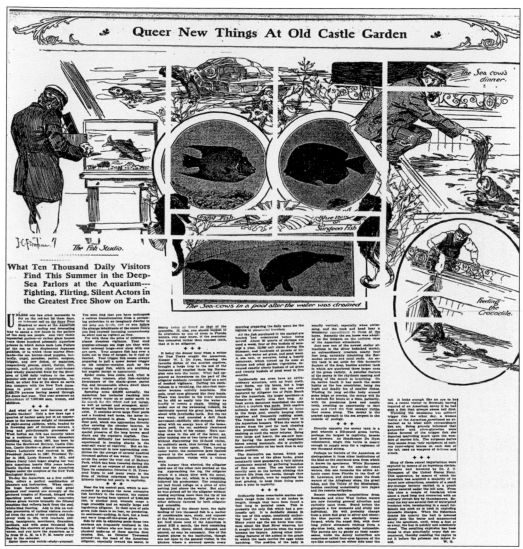

Queer New Things At Old Castle Garden

The Fish Studio.

The Sea cow's dinner.

Green Fish

Blue Ibis or Surgeon Fish

The Sea-cows in a pool after the water was drained

Feeding the Crocodile.

What Ten Thousand Daily Visitors Find This Summer in the Deep-Sea Parlors at the Aquarium--- Fighting, Flirting, Silent Actors in the Greatest Free Show on Earth.

THE AQUARIUM'S NEW EXHIBITS, 1905. In 1902, Dr. Charles H. Townsend became the aquarium's director and began improving the facility. By 1905, he had introduced new creatures, including sea cows, crocodiles, and surgeonfish. (New York Times.)

CHARLES HASKINS TOWNSEND. This portrait photograph of the director of the New York Aquarium was taken in 1888 when he was still with the United States Fish Commission. Dr. Charles H. Townsend (1859–1944) assumed his duties at Castle Garden in 1902 and retired in 1937. During his tenure, the New York Aquarium flourished as the leading municipal aquarium in the country. (Condor.)

A WILLIAM JENNINGS BRYAN POLITICAL RALLY. The Democratic presidential candidate is seen campaigning in Battery Park, around 1900.

quarium and Battery
ark, New York City.

THE AQUARIUM, 1917. In June 1917, Louis L. Mowbray, the assistant director, embarked on a major fish-gathering expedition to the Caribbean island of Grand Turk. However, shortly before his return to New York, a hurricane struck, and he lost many of the specimens.

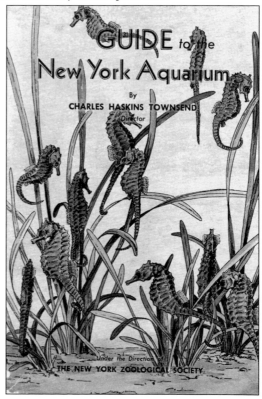

TOWNSEND'S GUIDEBOOK TO THE AQUARIUM. In 1919, Dr. Charles H. Townsend wrote this guide to the New York Aquarium. The volume was immensely popular and remained in print until the aquarium closed.

BATTERY PARK, 1920. This photograph shows the aquarium shortly before its enlargement.

AT THE NEW YORK AQUARIUM'S THRESHOLD, 1924. Attracting as many as two million visitors annually, the aquarium was popular with families, school groups, clubs, and tourists, as well as with ordinary New Yorkers. There was never a fee to pass over its threshold and enjoy the specimens on display.

INSIDE THE NEW YORK AQUARIUM, 1924. New York's aquarium was an elegant place, and under the intelligent and versatile guidance of Dr. Charles H. Townsend and such able assistants as Louis L. Mowbray and Charles M. Breder, the institution retained its popularity for as long as it was open. This is how the aquarium looked following the renovation that added upper stories to the building. The architectural firm of McKim, Mead, and White executed the design.

DR. CHARLES HASKINS TOWNSEND, 1926. The able guidance of Dr. Charles H. Townsend was felt everywhere throughout the aquarium and ensured its continued success. Earlier in his career, Dr. Townsend undertook important scientific work on whales and their habitat, as well as on tortoises of the Galapagos Islands. After his retirement in 1937, he and his family moved to Florida, where he died in 1944 at the age of 85.

VIEW OF THE BATTERY AND BAY FROM WALL STREET. This magnificent view from the financial district shows the Battery, the New York Aquarium at Castle Garden, the Statue of Liberty on Bedloe's Island, and the Ellis Island Immigrant Station. This picture was taken in the mid- or late 1920s.

THE SERVICE GALLERY. The large exhibition tanks could be conveniently serviced by members of the staff. On the right are the wooden reserved tanks. This was one of the areas hidden away from visitors, yet it was a secret world of great activity.

ELECTRICAL PUMP EQUIPMENT. The electrically powered pumps kept the water circulating in the aquarium's tanks. Pumps, piping, filters, reservoirs, air compressors, feed rooms, water heaters, and coolers were kept out of the sight of visitors.

THE SEAHORSE. This specially designed boat was used for collecting the aquarium's fish, which were stowed in a water compartment called a well. Built in 1920, the sloop was 35 feet long and had a power engine as well as a sail. It contained berths for four men.

MOONFISH. This specimen from the aquarium was a silvery moonfish. These fish are also called "moonyfish" or "fingerfish."

Sea Turtles. The creatures' swimming motions can be observed here.

The Bullfrog. The bullfrog is the largest of frogs, and, according to Dr. Charles H. Townsend, sometimes measured 17 inches from its snout to the toes in its hind legs. He remarked that it had a voracious appetite and was capable of leaping to a distance of seven feet.

GREETINGS FROM A 300-POUND GROUPER. Taken from the waters of Florida and the West Indies, groupers commonly weighed as much as 500 pounds; the one facing the camera here weighed more than 300 pounds.

ALLIGATOR FEEDING TIME. The aquarium had two alligators measuring eight feet long. The aquarium also kept crocodiles.

FRINGE-TAILED GOLDFISH. Natives to East Asia, lovely fringe-tailed goldfish are favorite ornamental fish for aquaria.

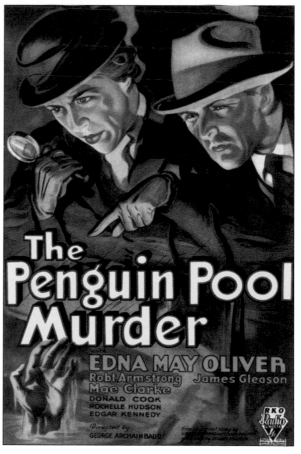

THE PENGUIN POOL MURDER. In this movie mystery, a body is found inside the New York Aquarium's penguin pool. Based on Stuart Palmer's 1931 mystery novel, the Hollywood film version was released in 1932 and starred Edna May Oliver as schoolmistress and amateur detective Hildegarde Withers. Her costar James Gleason played the bumbling detective, inspector Oscar Piper of the Homicide Bureau. Other leading members of the cast include Robert Armstrong, Mae Clark, and Clarence H. Wilson. Wilson portrayed the director of the aquarium.

THE SAND SHARK. This nine-foot-long sand shark survived in the aquarium for more than five years.

NAVY DAY, 1934. In May 1934, the navy visited New York and inevitably attracted a great throng to see the ships from the Battery.

Eight

THE SURVIVOR

THE DESTROYER ROBERT MOSES. In September–October 1941, city parks commissioner Robert Moses (left) closed the New York Aquarium, with plans to demolish it so that he could build the Brooklyn-Battery Tunnel. In 1942, he demolished the aquarium but delayed pulling down the heavy stone walls of Castle Garden due to the war and because it became clear that he could construct the tunnel without the need of destroying the old fortress. He is pictured here with New York governor Franklin D. Roosevelt.

DEMOLITION AND CLEANUP, 1950. Although this picture was taken after most of the structure was gone, it does give some idea of what New Yorkers were faced with after the needless destruction of the aquarium.

HARRY S. TRUMAN. Although Congress and Pres. Harry S. Truman approved legislation hastily declaring the old aquarium a national monument in 1946, the City of New York still owned the property, and the federal government could do nothing. A huge battle between Robert Moses and his allies on one side and preservationists and politicians (including Mayor William O'Dwyer, Gov. Thomas Dewey, and Sen. Robert F. Wagner) on the other ensued. Four years later, the state legislature and Governor Dewey finally ceded the landmark to Washington, and the federal legislation took effect on July 18, 1950.

RESTORATION. In the 1970s, the site was restored to its military appearance, and the National Park Service promoted its military past and its days as a showplace, immigrant station, and aquarium, through a permanent exhibit.

CASTLE CLINTON AND THE BATTERY. In 1986, the Circle Line ferryboat ticket office was moved to Castle Clinton. Since the tickets are for excursions to the Statue of Liberty and, beginning in 1990, Ellis Island, millions of tourists poured into the site each year. In 2005, the Castle Garden's immigration records were made available on the Internet at CastleGarden.org. This will prove to be an invaluable source to genealogists, historians, and researchers.

CASTLE GARDEN'S HALL OF FAME

Alexander Berkman (1870–1936)	Russia (Lithuania), 1888	Anarchist
Franz Boas (1858–1942)	Germany, 1886	Anthropologist
Edward Bok (1863–1930)	Holland, 1870	Pulitzer Prize–winning author
Mother Cabrini (1850–1917)	Italy, 1889	Nun, mother superior, missionary
James J. Davis (1873–1947)	Wales, 1881	U.S. senator, secretary of labor
William Fox (1879–1952)	Hungary, 1879	Founder, Twentieth Century Fox film studios
L. Wolfe Gilbert (1886–1971)	Russia, 1887	Songwriter, vaudevillian
Emma Goldman (1869–1940)	Russia, 1885	Anarchist
Samuel Gompers (1850–1924)	England, 1863	Trade union leader
Oscar Hammerstein (1846–1919)	Prussia (Germany), 1863	Theatrical impresario
Victor Herbert (1859–1924)	Ireland, 1886	Composer of operettas
Harry Houdini (1874–1926)	Hungary, 1886	Magician
Magnus Johnson (1871–1936)	Sweden, 1890	U.S. senator
Mary Mallon (1869–1937)	Ireland, 1883	Cook; known as Typhoid Mary
José Martí (1853–1895)	Cuba, 1880	Poet, journalist, revolutionary
Joseph Pulitzer (1847–1911)	Hungary, 1864	Newspaper publisher
Michael I. Pupin (1858–1935)	Serbia, 1874	physicist, inventor
Jacob A. Riis (1849–1914)	Denmark, 1870	Writer, photographer, social reformer
Charles P. Steinmetz (1865–1923)	Germany, 1889	Electrical engineer, inventor
Nikola Tesla (1856–1943)	Croatia, 1884	Scientist, inventor
Sophie Tucker (1884–1966)	Russia, 1884	Singer, vaudevillian
Robert F. Wagner (1877–1953)	Germany, 1886	U.S. senator
Adolph Zukor (1873–1976)	Hungary, 1888	Filmmaker, founder of Paramount Pictures

BIBLIOGRAPHY

Dolkart, Andrew S. "Castle Clinton." In *The Encyclopedia of New York City*, edited by Kenneth T. Jackson. New Haven, CT: Yale University Press, 1995.

Gilder, Rodman. *The Battery: The Story of Four Centuries on Manhattan's Tip.* Boston: Houghton Mifflin, 1936.

July, Robert W. *The Essential New Yorker: Gulian C. Verplanck.* Durham, NC: Duke University Press, 1951.

Kapp, Friedrich. *Immigration and the Commissioners of Emigration of the State of New York.* New York: The Nation Press, 1870.

Moreno, Barry. "Castle Garden: The Forgotten Gateway." *Ancestry*, April 2003.

———. "Castle Garden and the Old Immigration." In *Die Auswanderung nach Nordamerika aus den Regionen des heutigen Rheinland-Pfalz*, edited by Werner Kremp and Roland Paul. Atlantische Texte (Band 16). Trier, Germany: Wissenschaftlicher Verlag, 2002.

———. "Castle Garden und Ellis Island: Tore zu einer neuen Welt." In *Good Bye Bayern, Grüß Gott America: Auswanderung aus Bayern nach Amerika seit 1683*. Augsburg, Germany: Haus der Bayerischen Geschichte, 2004.

Novotny, Ann. *Strangers at the Door: Ellis Island, Castle Garden and the Great Mass Migration to America.* Riverside, CT: The Chatham Press, 1971.

Svejda, George. *Castle Garden as an Immigrant Depot, 1855–1890.* Washington, D.C.: United States Department of the Interior, National Park Service, 1968.

Townsend, Charles Haskins. *Guide to the New York Aquarium.* New York: Clark and Fritts, 1919.

———. *The Public Aquarium: Its Construction, Equipment and Management.* Washington, D.C.: United States Bureau of Fisheries, 1928.

INDEX

DISCOVER THOUSANDS OF LOCAL HISTORY BOOKS
FEATURING MILLIONS OF VINTAGE IMAGES

Arcadia Publishing, the leading local history publisher in the United States, is committed to making history accessible and meaningful through publishing books that celebrate and preserve the heritage of America's people and places.

Find more books like this at
www.arcadiapublishing.com

Search for your hometown history, your old stomping grounds, and even your favorite sports team.

Consistent with our mission to preserve history on a local level, this book was printed in South Carolina on American-made paper and manufactured entirely in the United States. Products carrying the accredited Forest Stewardship Council (FSC) label are printed on 100 percent FSC-certified paper.

MADE IN THE

USA